Acknowledgements

Thanks are due to a number of people who were involved in the production of this book:
to David Reynolds for all his hard work preparing the manuscript, to my wife Heather, Mike Darwood and Tim Jones for their help with various chapters and for proof reading, and to Lubna Sarwar for typing the original manuscripts.

❋ ❋ ❋

Dedication

This book is dedicated to all those men, women and children that I have had the privilege of seeing the Lord free from fear, depression, insecurity, stress, guilt, anxiety and failure, during 35 years of ministry.

BREAKTHROUGH into freedom

Conquering Depression anxiety and Fear

By Don Double

1 Time to Breakthrough

Part I
THE THINGS THAT BIND
2 Family Hurts
3 The Chains of Immorality
4 Dark Powers

Part II
FIND FREEDOM THAT LASTS
5 Freedom from Fear
6 Facing Failure
7 Break Free from Stress
8 Feeling Secure
9 You Can Do It!

CHAPTER 1

TIME TO BREAKTHROUGH

God's plan for your life is glorious freedom, if you are His child. Sadly, too many people live bound by the effects of their past, by fears and insecurities and totally miss out on the wonder of the freedom Jesus won for us. I have written this book because I believe that every Christian can and should be enjoying real freedom. If you are experiencing failure, guilt, anxiety, stress, depression or fear, this book is for you. It is time for you to breakthrough into freedom.

In Part One I am going to consider three fundamental areas that are breeding grounds for failure, depression, fear and their associated conditions. I have been involved in counselling and praying for many Christians who remain bound in areas of their lives through occult influences, sexual hang-ups and more than anything else, by the results of family breakdowns. My heart's desire is to see everyone in the Kingdom come to fully understand that *"the truth shall make you free"* (JOHN 8:32)

I really believe that too many Christians are not being shown how to throw off their past, and all the clutter that has become attached to them during their lives up to the day of conversion. The aim of the first three chapters is to show you how you can become influenced by your sinful actions and the deliberate or accidental actions of others. Then we will see how the Word of God, applied to your situation, can bring release and relief, enabling you to breakthrough into freedom for the future.

Part Two is titled 'Find Freedom that Lasts'. In it I want to look at some of the things people experience when they are suffering from damage due to their past. My aim is to highlight issues where you as a Christian need to be strong, and to provide you with godly answers and godly disciplines that will help you deal with your current predicament. God wants the best for all His children, please believe right now that you are His beloved child, whatever you may have done or had done to you! The best is clearly revealed in His Word: peace, joy, prosperity, the power of the Holy Spirit, perseverance, gentleness, a long life, children and grandchildren, strength, security, self-control, love. If you are not experiencing these and more (this list is not complete by any means), you are being robbed! Do not let this situation continue, reclaim the rightful inheritance due to you while you are on the earth.

Lastly, I would encourage you to pray right now before you begin to read this book. Ask God to clearly and gently show you areas where you need ministry, where to find the support you may need in dealing with issues that emerge, but most importantly, to reveal Himself to you in a fresh and personal way.

❋ ❋ ❋

Part One
THE THINGS THAT BIND

CHAPTER 2

FAMILY HURTS

The first area I wish to look at is the break up of the home. The home is the God-ordained environment in which we can live and grow up in safety, surrounded by warmth and love. God created the family; the first blessing recorded in Genesis is upon the man and woman to *"be fruitful and multiply"*. (GENESIS 1:28)

God is a Father, He has a Son, He has a home and He has a family—us! He also takes up a great deal of His Word talking about family, relationships, responsibilities and roles. So, we must not be surprised if Satan does all he can to destroy it, and it is clear from a casual glance at any newspaper today that the home is indeed under strong attack. Now, I believe that a direct result of the collapse of the original family unit is seen in the increase of depression in our country.

During the past few years I have been to Africa on several occasions yet I have not met many depressed people out in the bush. They may live in mud huts with none of the modern conveniences that our society considers to be essential, but we need to remember that 'mod cons' do not turn a house into a home. But love does! The African household is usually an extended family, including grandparents and great grandparents, living as a closely knit unit. This is one of the finest defences against depression that I know of.

When a House is not a Home
When there is love inside a person, there is also love on the outside, because real love cannot help but demonstrate itself physically, for example with a hug. The Bible say's, *"let us not love in word or in tongue, but in deed and in truth"*. (1 JOHN 3:18)

Some people tell me they cannot express love. My reply to that is that they should ask God to set them free so that they can. I believe that consequently this would set many people free from depression and anxiety too. I have spent many hours counselling depressed people, trying to get them to speak just one positive statement to say that they loved someone. However, some people cannot even think of one single person they have loved, or who they know accepts them and wants them for their own sake. Such people may have spent all their lives seeking acceptance. They have longed for it and have been constantly looking for it. When you listen to them, using the gift of discernment, you soon come to realise that they are constantly seeking to win your acceptance and by probing you, to find out whether you are accepting them or not.

However, with some gentle persuasion and the Holy Spirit pinpointing areas in their lives, they will eventually be able to remember some positive event from their past. Now, when that happens, I can usually see the depression begin to lift off them straight away. I will then encourage them to show love to someone in a practical way. My goal is to encourage them to commit themselves to making a constructive change in their attitude, and express it through a positive act of love.

I believe that one of the major things which has contributed to the mess families are in today is television. In the past families were used to sitting around the fire, talking or playing games, where their lives would be built together. Today, because we have televisions, people seem to go off to their rooms and shut the door. They have not learned how to have conversations with one another. Of course children do have to do their homework, but many have televisions and stereos in their bedrooms and so spend their free time there too. In fact, in many homes, although people live in the same house, their lives are completely separate, leading to loneliness and even resentment. A particularly crucial time for relationships to be built with your children is when they are teenagers. Parents with teenagers need to spend time and effort establishing good relationships. This is so that when they have children themselves, they will instinctively follow the same patterns. I stay in other people's homes as much as I stay in my own, and one of the saddest things I find is that in many homes there is a man with the title of father, but the last thing he is doing is being a father because there is little or no relationship between him and his children. Being a 'father' is all about having an active, daily relationship with your children, it is not about having a title.

Because I have a child, it does not give me the right to be called 'father'. What I do have, though, is the responsibility to become a father. But, unless I work it out daily in relationship with my children, I will never father them. Sadly, a father refusing to take up this responsibility can often cause depression in children and particularly teenagers for whom the lack of a strong paternal relationship can be really damaging. Serious medical conditions such as Anorexia Nervosa have been known to result from this form of neglect.

I have often had teenagers come up to me and ask for a 'daddy-hug' because they know what I am like with my children. They do this because they do not get physical affection from their own fathers. If you have felt convicted while reading this, I want to tell you that God wants you to be a real father to your children from this time onwards, and He wants to have a real Father/son relationship with you too. So, get out your Bible and a concordance, and do a study on the word 'father'. If you are prepared to put in some overtime with your children, you can make up for the pain, the anxiety and all the lost years.

There was a man who went home from one of our 'Men for God Conferences' and openly confessed his faults as a father and spouse. He then firmly laid down the new parameters the Lord had shown him for family life, and took up the reins of father and husband. Within a matter of hours, his wife had gladly handed over the mantle of leader she had been forced to wear, and within a few days the children had forgotten the old dad and were relishing the new. It can be done.

Childhood Roots

An unhappy childhood can produce deep hurts and feelings of rejection that can often lead to depression either then or in later life. A child may exhibit fairly obvious signs to a trained eye, but can also hide the feelings of pain and rejection deep down. In later life an adult might not know that the root of a behavioural problem or addiction, for example, was through rejection they experienced as a child. One typical scenario is that a family is beginning to break up but the parents go on struggling in order to stay together 'for the sake of the children'. However, because they never seek any help, the tension increases and becomes ever more unbearable.

Perhaps the curse of the 90's, as far as the family is concerned, is the acceptance, as normal, of models of family life that are less than God's best. In some cases people have been openly disobedient to His word, for instance, suggesting that it is OK for lesbian or homosexual couples to be parents together. I absolutely disagree! The Bible states clearly that God's plan was for a husband and wife team to raise a family. Even the large number of 'single parent' families cannot be considered as ideal in terms of God's best, even though many cannot help finding themselves separated from their partners and do a wonderful job as best they can. The truth is, that divorce hurts people, and not just the parents but the children as well. I have to counsel and pray with many people who, as adults, cry out in pain and tears, "Why did my mum and dad break up, why did it happen to me?"

Children need security. We all do. But many people do not realise that this does not come through receiving possessions but through knowing that they are loved. I know that God loves me of course, but just as important is the fact that my wife, children and members of my team all love me too. Let me tell you right now that this assurance gives me a wonderful feeling of security. Just to know that these people want me for my own sake is a great defence against fear and depression.

If you have not got a secure group of friends and family though; please remember that you do have Jesus. Think about the family situations He faced: He was illegitimate in the world's eyes; He was made homeless when Joseph and Mary had to flee to Egypt; He knew what it was to have a step-father; He had people trying to kill Him when He was a baby and when He took up His public ministry, and He had a family that did not understand Him. He's been there, and He cares for you.

Sadly, many parents create totally unnecessary fears and anxieties in their children. It's understandable that you want them to do well, get on, pass exams with a high grade and maybe go to college or university. So, when they do well, you give them a big present and encourage them. But if they do not do well, do you put them down? If you do, be aware that this can sow seeds of covetousness and envy between siblings, that can produce dreadful battles in families in later years. When one of my children failed an exam, I bought them a present because I wanted them to know that their dad was with them, that I still loved them and that it made no difference to our relationship whether they passed or failed. This is how you can deal with the roots of this sort of problem.

Hiding Behind Masks

When a home breaks up, trust and security will very often disappear. When you meet people who have been hurt in this way they very often put up barriers, or, to put it another way, they put on masks and it is hard work trying to relate to a mask. The reason for the mask is the wearer fears being hurt again; because of this they are not prepared to let God, you or anyone else into the hurt parts of their lives. However, the Bible clearly says that we should *"Bear one another's burdens, and so fulfill the Law of Christ."* (GALATIANS 6:2) You may think that you could never talk about what you've got hidden in your memory to another living soul, but let me tell you, *"There is nothing new under the sun."* (ECCLESIASTES 1:9)

Somebody else has been there before you and had to let someone into their secret. I promise you that if you ask the Lord to make sure you find the right person to help you, they will not be so shocked that they will reject or despise you. They will just love you more for your openness and integrity, and praise God that you have reached the place where you want to give up your intolerable burden. I can tell you, I have been to that place many times, because it's the same for everyone whose desire is to walk closely with the Lord. He purifies us all in the same way, and I believe it's one of the reasons He has put us in community with others, in family and church, so that we can help one another through these difficult times. People often try really hard to make you believe what they want you to believe about them. For instance, I have been told amazing stories about a person's wonderful dad, when in reality he abused them when they were young. They are afraid that you will discover who they really are and reject them, so they hide behind a mask. If that is your situation, I beg you to lay that mask down and let God and His people come into your life. Find love and security in their acceptance. Jesus can release you from every fear, bad experience, sense of guilt, feeling of uncleanliness and knowledge of rejection.

The whole issue of rejection can be a breeding ground for insecurity and resentment. If you are rejected, you are always looking around to see whether or not people accept you. I had the same problem but now I could not care less whether or not people accept me. I know I am loved by the most important person in the universe, Jesus.

Some people, when you tell them they have a bondage of rejection and that God wants to set them free, turn round and say, "I am rejected but it is the other person who has the problem because they rejected me". This is not entirely true. The other person may have a problem and of course they should not have rejected you. At the same time though, you have a bondage and need to be healed and set free from it.

The Root of Bitterness

One of the deep problems that comes out of all the issues I have been raising is that we can grow bitter and resentful. The truth is that while this bitterness and resentment remains, we can never be completely set free. No amount of psychiatric or medical help will work on hurts that have a spiritual root, so without the Lord's help we could remain depressed for the rest of our lives.

A picture from nature will help to show what I mean. If your problems and bad behaviour are the leaves and the branches of a tree, they will continue to flourish while the root is healthy. You could spend a lifetime sweeping up messy piles of leaves and twigs. When the roots of the tree are dug up though, everything will be dealt with at the same time and the whole tree can be thrown into the fire. Bitterness is a spiritual issue and God tells us to be on our guard, *"Looking diligently lest anyone should fall short of the grace of God; lest any root of bitterness springing up should cause trouble, and by this many become defiled."* (HEBREWS 12:15)

I believe God is speaking to two groups of people here. He is not only exhorting those who recognise any resentment in their lives to get it sorted out, but is also reminding the rest of us to be on the lookout for signs of bitterness in the lives of other Christians and when we recognise it, to help them come through it.

Bitterness often begins with a sour relationship, in fact some people I have counselled have carried resentment towards someone for over thirty years. So, the crucial thing you need to do, so far as the Lord is concerned, is to forgive. You may feel that you can never forgive the person who hurt you, but by the grace of God you can. I have had to do it and I think that just about every Christian who wants to grow further with the Lord has had to do it. It is hard, but this is where the support of a wise and mature friend is so helpful. Whether it is hard or not, the Lord commands us to forgive! *"For if you forgive men when they sin against you, your heavenly Father will also forgive you. But if you do not forgive men their sins, your Father will not forgive your sins."* (MATTHEW 6:14-15)

Loneliness

The Bible states clearly, that *"it is not good that man should be alone".* (GENESIS 2:18)

My definition of loneliness is a lack of a deep relationship with anyone. Some people can experience loneliness when they are in a room full of people, because it is not caused by being in a deserted place, but by not feeling welcomed by people you have not met before. You can be married, live in the same house, eat at the same table, raise children together, even sleep in the same bed and still be utterly lonely. I believe that the only answer is to take the mask off, open yourself up, let your spouse and children into your life, and let family relationships become what they should be. Above everything else, let Jesus Christ come completely into your life. Jesus is in love with you, just let yourself fall in love with Him.

Love is something that everyone longs for but few find. Love is not the same thing as having sex, though for a married couple that may be the outcome of a day of loving each other and is a beautiful thing. The media will often present love in a way that would be better expressed as lust, which is why so many young people get such a warped idea of what true love really is. Love has to be based on a real, honest, selfless relationship. Love is sacrificial. Love is completely unconditional. Love is the giving of yourself completely to another person. Love is not just a nice feeling. Paul puts it like this, *"Love suffers long and is kind; love does not envy; love does not parade itself, is not puffed up; does not behave rudely, does not seek its own, is not provoked, thinks no evil; does not rejoice in iniquity, but rejoices in the truth; bears all things, believes all things, hopes all things, endures all things. Love never fails."* (1 CORINTHIANS 13:4-8)

As I have already mentioned, I have relationships where I know that people love me to the extent that whatever they discovered about me, they would still love me and care for me. That is the kind of love that casts out fear. There should be a commitment in godly love that means you will stick by your brother whatever you find out about him. You see, when we discover real love, fear goes! *"There is no fear in love, but perfect love casts out fear because fear involves torment, but he who fears has not been made perfect in love."*(1 JOHN 4:18)

I hope that I have thrown some light on issues where you need to let the Lord come in and bring His healing and forgiveness. The most important point that I would like to re-emphasise is that of forgiveness. I have written a small guide on the subject of forgiveness which I would heartily recommend to you if you are struggling to say "I forgive you". There may be some things that happened to you in the past for which you must forgive those who were responsible, completely and unconditionally, just as God forgives you when you repent of your sins. Unforgiveness is such a destructive root. If you find it really hard, ask a Christian friend to come alongside and pray with you.

CHAPTER 3

THE CHAINS OF IMMORALITY

The second thing I want us to look at is the area of sexual immorality as a major cause of guilt, depression, emotional breakdown, behavioural problems and insecurity. The biblical terms for the immoral practises condemned by God are fornication and adultery, bestiality[1] and homosexuality.[2] Do not let anyone tell you that the last one is a chemical/hormone condition, because the Bible clearly say's it's sin. But God can deal with it! You can find God's views on the different types of immorality in Leviticus 18 & 20 and Romans 1:24-27.

If God says it is sin, the only thing you can do is to accept it and believe what He says. You see, He is right every time, and whatever we believe He will not change and even if a Bishop or Archbishop says differently, the Word of God still says, *"Forever, O LORD, your word is settled in heaven."* (PSALMS 119:89)

All the things that I am referring to can cause depression, and even emotional breakdowns, sometimes many years after the event. When two people have intercourse, something happens that is more than a physical encounter. The Bible clearly states that when a man and a woman sleep together *"the two shall become one flesh."* (1 CORINTHIANS 6:16B)

In other words, something happens in the soul realm. 1 Corinthians 6:16 is a quotation from Genesis 2:24 (look it up if you've never seen it before), where God establishes the principles for sexual behaviour for the whole of humankind. At a casual glance Genesis 2:24 is an insignificant verse, but it has so many implications for men and women that it warrants some thorough study. I have not got the space to write more fully here, but let me condense it into a few words. Becoming one flesh means being joined in soul and body, totally, inextricably, permanently. That was God's

---
[1] Bestiality; I have included bestiality because the Lord put it alongside the other more prevalent sexual sins, and also because it does happen today.
[2] Homosexuality; please understand that what we refer to as lesbianism, the Bible calls homosexuality. It's the same term for both men and women.

plan for men and women, a union for life!

I believe that it is impossible to function properly as a Christian when you are 'one flesh' with two or more people simultaneously. It is the tension that this causes, especially when you have no idea of the implications of what you have done, that can lead to some very deep problems. It is a sobering thought to think that there are unbelieving men and women who have had hundreds of sexual partners, and that they are all joined, or soul-tied, to one other. Some of the most severe causes of depression I have ever seen have had their roots in an illicit sexual relationship. But, recognition of the problem is only the first stage of the process. I have heard of women who have been 'joined' to over two hundred partners, through promiscuous behaviour when they were young, and the Lord has freed them totally.

Praise the Lord, then, that He is able and willing to break the ties you may have made before you became a Christian. God's pattern in Genesis 2 is the best, so do not feel guilt-ridden because of your past, but repent and ask for His forgiveness and cleansing, so you may experience His best from now onwards.

Definitions
Of the list of immoral practices listed at the beginning of the chapter, two words perhaps need some clarification because they are not commonly used today. Fornication is defined as sex outside marriage; so, sex between courting couples, engaged couples, boyfriends and girlfriends, holiday flings and one night stands all come into this category. Adultery is defined as occurring when one of, or both, the couple are married to someone else. Another point is that there is no such thing as 'making love' in the Bible; the emotional nature of the joining does not turn the sinful act into a righteous one. In fact, whatever the emotional nature of the experience, it is the emotional nature afterwards that is much more important—guilt!

I know one lady who was saved and became a member of a good church but her husband, an extremely successful and wealthy businessman, remained unconverted. He suddenly declared his intention of arranging an illicit weekend with another couple. She refused at first, but after several months she bowed to the enormous pressure he was exerting and agreed to this wife-swapping weekend. Up to this point she had been a healthy stable person, but immediately afterwards she began to go to pieces and finished up in a psychiatric hospital with a severe breakdown.

She wrote to her pastor from the hospital for help. She had been subjected to Electroshock Therapy, drugs and psychiatric analysis but none of these things had been of any real help to her because none of them could cleanse her from her guilt. Some counselling took place, but when her husband heard of it he forbade her from seeing any person who was a Christian. He could see it was guilt that was destroying her, but thought it was a form of religious pressure that had generated it. Little did he know that it was a serious spiritual condition caused by his own actions. There was no way to help her further. The truth is that psychiatric help can only go so far. It is the blood of Jesus shed on the cross at Calvary that is the only means of release from guilt.

The Strength to Say No

I want to tell you that one of the most beautiful things you can ever do is to stand before God, and the Minister, on the day you get married knowing that you are a virgin. You may be unpopular at your school or college by making a stand, but I tell you, it's worth it. I do appreciate that the pressures are enormous today. I personally know a young lady who, when she started university, received a letter from the university telling her where to buy condoms. With it was a note saying, 'Remember you are here to experiment'!

God's desire is to help you exert all your will in this area and to exercise self control. If you see it as a test of your faith, remember that the Bible say's that, *"No temptation has overtaken you except such as is common to man; but God is faithful, who will not allow you to be tempted beyond what you are able, but with the temptation will also make the way of escape, that you may be able to bear it."* (1 CORINTHIANS 10:13)

I believe the 'way of escape' is the hunger to be obedient to the Word and make God pleased with your faithfulness. Also, share your burden with an older and wiser married person of your own sex, so you can be accountable and they can support and encourage you all the way up to your wedding day.

19

Let me tell you about a couple whom we met at one of GNC's Camps several years ago. They were living together but were not married, so we told them to put a stop to it. They got right with God, went home and were married soon after. The result was a complete transformation in their relationship. God really blessed their marriage and they are now completely sold out for Him, giving Him the glory for rescuing them from a sinful life into one of real freedom in Jesus. This can be your experience too, if you face up to your sin and bring it to the cross.

Sin is Sin

Let me state two further things; I have been shocked to see many born-again Christians, some of them even Spirit-filled, openly say that to preach no to sex before marriage is old fashioned. I want to tell you that it is not old fashioned, it is as up-to-date as the Word of God. It is God's will and therefore it is already set for tomorrow and you cannot be more modern than that. Secondly, do not think that by getting married you have legalised any fornication you committed beforehand. It is sin, even after 50 years of marriage and the death of your spouse, and as such it still needs repenting of.

Let me give you an example of what I mean. A lady came to me for help, explaining that she had a problem that expressed itself as a compulsion to regularly wash her hands. Her marriage was in real trouble and her Church, a loving and caring one, had been unable to help. She just could not come through into victory.

As she shared her problem with me, I told her that the Lord was showing me that it was the result of something that had happened to her as a teenager. With this she opened up and told me the whole story. When she was a teenager, she had been involved in an act of fornication. Immediately afterwards she had felt unclean and filthy. Since that time she had been trying to get herself clean by washing her hands. We immediately prayed together, she repented of her sin, and the blood of Jesus washed all the guilt away. She was set completely free!

The Consequences for the 1990's

The 'sexual revolution' of the 1960's was responsible for a great deal of damage to our society. However, I believe that what we are experiencing today is much, much worse. Permissiveness creeps steadily on each year, so that we become immune to the gradual and subtle decline in moral standards.

What passes for entertainment, is often simply toned down pornography. '18' rated horror and sex videos are being watched by youngsters, who hire them from shops flagrantly breaking the Law. The media as a whole provides editorial space for gays and lesbians to promote their views and their work. This whole scenario has worn down the acceptable levels of behaviour that used to be in place. We must pray that the Lord protects us and our children from the effects of so-called 'freedom' in the 1990's.

It is quite common now to hear that junior school children suffer from severe nightmares from the 'adult' films they have watched and been unable to cope with. In fact so many children are really not allowed to be children today because of the enormous pressures on them to grow up so fast and 'conform to the pattern of this world'.

One of the most debilitating and degrading experiences shared by more and more women is the dreadful crime of rape. The guilt and depression felt by victims can, if not brought to the Lord, be carried for a lifetime of grief and bitterness. When the victim is in the care of Christians who are committed to helping her, the most important areas that need dealing with are forgiving the guilty party and letting the tender love of God into every wounded area of the body, soul and spirit.

Let's look briefly at HIV and AIDS. A lot has been spoken about the origins of the disease, but for me it is a question of, "it's here, so how do we deal with it, as Christians?" I have seen people completely healed from AIDS, praise the Lord! I fully expected to see such healings and now they are happening. Also, people are being converted to Christ because of the terrible situation they have found themselves in. So, whether or not people are being healed, one of my favourite sayings is as applicable here to AIDS sufferers, as with everyone else. 'You can get into heaven with a sick body, but you can't with a sin-sick soul'.

If you know someone with HIV or AIDS, treat them like anyone else who needs salvation. Get alongside them, show them Jesus by your behaviour, attitudes and character. Bring them to the Lord! If they get healed that is great, but if not at least they will know eternal life rather than eternal torment. The healing of the emotional consequences of having AIDS should be dealt with in exactly the same way as the other examples in this chapter. Remember, God wants to free you from drug abuse, and its associated problems like theft and lying. He wants to turn around your homosexual desires and replace them with the heterosexual ones he established between Adam and Eve. He wants you in His Kingdom!

I am amazed by the the number of people I have ministered to over the years who have been permanently delivered and set free from all sorts of fears, anxieties, worries, hurts and guilt-trips through coming to Jesus and repenting of sexual sin. Whatever you feel now, let me assure you that there is nothing that you have done that cannot be forgiven, cleansed by the blood of Jesus and completely healed. If God has revealed areas of sin in your life which need to be dealt with, I would encourage you to ask a mature Christian friend to pray with you as soon as possible. You should repent straightaway and receive His complete forgiveness and healing:

1. Repentance is the key to God's cleansing and forgiveness.
2. Every sin is washed clean through the Blood of Jesus, through His sacrificial work on the cross.
3. There is no condemnation for those who are in Christ Jesus.
4. The Love of God can heal every hurt, guilt, pain, depression, trauma or whatever else you may have experienced because of what happened in your past.

We are living in wicked times, the pressures upon us to 'follow the crowd' are enormous, but Jesus came to give us the victory over the desires of the flesh. Stand firm on the Word, get to know Jesus better and love your Father with everything you've got. Then you will *"be able to withstand in the evil day, and having done all, to stand"*. (EPHESIANS 6:13)

CHAPTER 4

DARK POWERS

The third breeding ground for depression I want to consider is contact with the occult. I have found during my years of ministry that many cases of fear, depression and severe behavioural problems are rooted in various kinds of occult activity. Seemingly (to the world anyway) harmless 'games' such as playing the Ouija board have lead to suicide attempts. Attending a séance, reading a horoscope or having your fortune told can have equally devastating consequences. These things are not harmless jokes, they are deadly dangerous! For instance, some people say to me, "Mr Double, I read my horoscope but I do not believe it". That is not true. I believe that everyone who reads their horoscope is hoping to find out that something good is going to happen to them during the day. If what they read is not good they try to forget it, but a seed has been sown in their heart and it can affect them all day long, and sometimes for much longer.

Do Not Touch
Satan knows that there is in each of us what has been described as a God shaped hole, that only God can fill. When God is denied access there, people still retain an instinctive hunger for the supernatural and this gives the opportunity for the enemy to make his move. This can lead to all sorts of occult activities such as those that I have mentioned or, even more seriously, involvement in black or white magic. All occult practice is expressly forbidden in the Bible. *"There shall not be found among you anyone who makes his son or his daughter pass through the fire, or one who practices witchcraft, or a soothsayer, or one who interprets omens, or a sorcerer, or one who conjures spells, or a medium, or a spiritist, or one who calls up the dead, for all who do these things are an abomination to the Lord".* (DEUTERONOMY 18:10-12)

23

Also, before you say 'ah, but...', let me tell you that astrology and Ouija are both soothsaying activities covered by this list from Deuteronomy 18. The Lord regards them all equally seriously and the Bible warns us on fifty occasions against involvement and contact with the occult. (If you want clarification on any other activity you may be worried about, wondering if it has an occult root, please write to me at the address at the back of this book).

The good news of the Kingdom, though, is that the blood of Christ is totally effective in breaking the power of Satan over a person's life and setting the captive free. However, there has to be specific confession and repentance when God shows us something from our past that He wants to deal with. Then, when we ask Him to set us free He will do so. If as you read this you become aware of any occult activities in your past that have not been dealt with, bring them before God and ask Him to set you free right now. It might be helpful for you to contact your pastor or another trusted counsellor and ask them to pray with you.

In Jesus' Name
If you are troubled by any activity of Satan, whether it is outside or inside you, your first desire should be to get rid of it by commanding it to go "in the name of Jesus". You can be set free from the power of demons in the name of Jesus! All 'enemy activity' in our lives must go, because the name of Jesus has absolute authority over everything, both in Heaven and in Hell and on the earth. Let me add that I believe there does not need to be a manifestation, such as screaming, when these things are being dealt with. Our guide in all matters of ministry is Jesus, and when He spoke to some demons saying, *"be quiet and come out of him"* (MARK 1:25), they left quietly because they had no other choice. Although others did come out shouting and screaming, the point I am making is we have the authority to keep the demonic quiet so that God gets all the attention, not His enemy. In fact, we speak with all the weight and authority of Jesus on our lips when we speak "in His name".

God Turns it Around
I have already mentioned some occult activities earlier in the chapter and

I would also include freemasonry in this category. From my experience of praying with people, it is clear that freemasonry can commonly cause depression and fear in people's lives. Also, even a basic look at some of the initiation rituals reveals things that are blatantly contrary to the teachings of the Bible. Despite this, many men who are involved deny that there is anything occult about freemasonry. People who are themselves freemasons, as well as those who have Masonic activity in their forefathers' lives, can suffer from its effects.

At the end of some of our missions we ask people to bring all their occult paraphernalia to be burnt (see Acts 19:19). I remember on one occasion a man came along who was the master of the local lodge and God had spoken to him during one of our meetings. He brought his cape, with great solid silver lapels that must have been worth hundreds of pounds, and joyfully burnt it in the fire. Praise the Lord that he was set free that day from all the effects of freemasonry in his life. If there has been any Masonic influence, or any other occult activity, in your family, it is important that you make sure you're completely free from its effects.

Where Does it Come From?

When looking at the spirit realm, the most important thing is to know the source of the activity. In Acts 16, the people were being told by a fortune teller that "these are the servants of the Most High God", referring to Paul and Silas. This was as accurate as you can get, they were indeed the servants of the Most High God. What was wrong was the source that the information was coming from. It was not coming from God's Holy Spirit but from an evil spirit. In the end Paul got so angry that he turned round and said to the spirit, *"I command you in the name of the Lord Jesus to come out of her"*. (ACTS 16:18)

The spirit left her immediately, so that she could not tell fortunes any more, and the people who used to make money out of her were very angry and put Paul and Silas in prison. Even though they had been badly whipped, Paul and Silas had a prayer meeting in the middle of the night and the famous result was, of course, that God sent an earthquake and they were sprung from captivity. The next thing we know they were having a crusade in the gaoler's home and every member of the family got saved!

The important thing to remember about occult activities is that God forbids us from having anything to do with them. If in doubt do not touch! Seek the advice of wise and mature Christian friends, or do a Bible study on the subject. Some people have been affected when their father, or another close relative, has been involved in occult activities in the past, such as freemasonry. If this is something you are aware of, just come before the Lord and repent, asking God to cleanse you from any occult activity that was established beyond your control. Remember, Satan is defeated! Jesus has already won the victory through his death and resurrection! It is this sacrificial work by our Lord that is the sole means by which we can experience release from these types of activities.

Part Two

FIND FREEDOM THAT LASTS

CHAPTER 5

FREEDOM FROM FEAR

"I sought the Lord and He heard me and delivered me from all my fears." (PSALM 34:4)
"In all your ways know, recognise and acknowledge Him, and He will direct and make straight and plain your paths. Be not wise in your own eyes; reverently fear and worship the Lord, and turn entirely away from evil. It shall be health to your nerves and sinews, and marrow and moistening to your bones". (PROVERBS 3:6-8, THE AMPLIFIED BIBLE)

God Has The Answer
I believe that God has the answer to every one of the casualties of today's society and the answer is Jesus. At the beginning of His ministry, Jesus said, *"The Spirit of the Lord is upon me, because He has anointed me to preach the gospel to the poor, He has sent me to heal the broken hearted, to preach deliverance to the captives and recovery of sight to the blind, to set at liberty those who are oppressed, to preach the acceptable year of the Lord."* (LUKE 4:18-19)

Note that Jesus said that "the Spirit of the Lord was upon Him"; the same Holy Spirit is upon us today, because His ministry has not changed. He equips us to do exactly what Jesus did and even greater things too. (John 14:12)

One of the problem areas listed in Luke 4 is being oppressed, which literally means 'crushed by cruel oppression', and that is exactly what depression does; it crushes! Another way to express this is to say a person has been 'bruised'. In fact the Bible exactly sums up one way Jesus paid the price, *"He was bruised for our iniquities".* (ISAIAH 53:5)

Physical bruising can be very painful. I remember that during one crusade I shut my finger in the lid of a piano, severely bruising it. Afterwards I commented that I expected to lose my finger nail, but a

29

member of my team said, "let's pray and ask God to heal it". As a result I did not lose the nail and God took the bruising away very quickly. But, while I had my bruise it caused me a lot of pain. In the same way, there are many people who feel deep pain inside from emotional damage they have received, but the good news is that the Lord can deal with your internal bruises as easily and quickly as He healed my externally bruised finger.

I am so glad that my God does not bruise or crush anyone. The Psalmist says, *"But you, O Lord, are a shield for me, my glory and the One who lifts up my head".* (PSALMS 3:3)

Likewise, Jesus quotes from Isaiah saying, *"A bruised reed He will not break, and a smoking flax He will not quench, till He sends forth justice to victory."* (MATTHEW 12:20)

If you feel crushed today, turn to Jesus and He will lift up your head. I can go anywhere with my head held high, because Jesus has lifted it up. God is a lifter, and if you call on the name of the Lord today, He will do the same for you.

Jesus v the Medical Condition

One of the recurring illnesses of the last thirty years has been nervous disorder. The verses I used at the beginning of the chapter tell us that we can have healthy nerves (Proverbs 3:6-8, The Amplified Bible), and that should be our goal. We will get healthy nerves as a result of fearing God, reverently worshipping Him with all our heart and turning entirely from evil. That is simple isn't it? It does not take a two-year course of pills or two teaspoons of mixture three times a day! Neither pills nor any other medicine can make you fear God and turn from evil. God's word, the 'Gos-pill', is the answer to the problem of nerves, but it is not the answer that many people want to hear. For some, it is far too simple.

I am not seeking to belittle the work of doctors in any way. When they seek to heal the sick they are doing the will of God, whether they realise it or not, but there are limits to what they can do with the aid of medicines. My own doctor summed it up when I met him sometime ago and he asked me how my work was going. After we had talked for a few minutes he said, "Mr Double, you can do more for half the people who come to my surgery than I can; their basic problem is that they do not have anything to believe in". I am sure that my doctor's comment was absolutely true. People who do not have a real, solid faith in something on which to base their lives are a target for fears, anxieties, depression and tension.

For many people who live on a diet of fear and worry, the result can eventually be depression. One way the medical world has tried to deal with depression is through drugs. Unfortunately, the consequences of doctors failing to understand the spiritual dimension in man are not good. Approximately 1¼ million people are chronic tranquilliser users (Benzodiazepine) in the UK today, and of them, two thirds are women over fifty years old. Although GP's have stopped prescribing the drug to new patients in recent years, many people are suffering because they had already become addicts.

Phobias are another major cause of suffering today, where one of the most common is claustrophobia, the fear of enclosed spaces. Let me tell you about a sufferer of agoraphobia, the fear of open spaces. A woman with this complaint came into the tent during one of my crusades and received ministry. The next morning as I walked through the town, I heard my name being called. When I looked up, the same woman was across the street waving to me and shouting, "Look at me Mr Double, I am out all by myself". The Lord had healed her and as a result her husband got saved too. Today he is an Elder in a local Brethren Assembly.

Another manifestation of anxiety is the inability to sleep properly. Sadly, many people suffer from insomnia which can be directly related to the things they fear. I remember a mission where there happened to be many sufferers. I ministered on the subject one Saturday evening and on the Sunday a man came up to me and said, "Mr Double, my wife and I were late for church this morning". I wondered what it had to do with me, but asked him what had happened. He explained that he never had any difficulty in sleeping but that his wife was a chronic sufferer from insomnia. However, she had attended the evening meeting on the Saturday and when she went to bed that night she had gone straight to sleep. She did not wake up until 9.30 on Sunday morning and neither did he!

A Royal Testimony

From our opening quotation from Psalm 34, and many other Psalms too, we learn that David was a man who at one time suffered from many fears. In his distress, however, he did not look for a doctor, he sought the Lord. If you suffer from fear, depression, anxiety attacks or a nervous disposition, then follow a King's example and seek the Lord now. The next part of David's testimony is so encouraging, because we have access to the same source of strength and healing. When David sought the Lord, God heard him. When we seek God He hears us! Our God is among us. Many people have problems because their God is so far away. They fail to locate Him where He really is—right there with them.

Not only did God hear David, He also delivered him; the God that I am writing about goes into action whenever He hears us. At this point, many people reading Psalm 34 seem to get the words confused and think they are reading, 'and delivered me from **some** of my fears'. That is not what the Psalmist says, nor what my Bible says. Spurgeon, in his commentary on the Psalms 'The Treasury of David', puts it beautifully when he stresses that the little word **all** means exactly what it says; I can assure you now that all does not mean every fear except the one that you have. It includes that one too. This is a tremendous foundation for faith for people with fears.

All the problems we have been thinking about are interrelated and they all have a cause. They do not just happen. The root cause of every one of them is a fear of one kind or another. Let me assure you that whatever the cause of your problem, Jesus is the answer. I would encourage all my readers who are suffering from one of these conditions rooted in a fear to really settle it in their hearts that they are going to seek the Lord, and to believe that He will deliver them. Come to the place where you see your fear for what it is, but only so that you can be delivered from it.

Positive v Negative

I often describe fear as faith in reverse gear. God has given every one of us the ability to believe Him, *"as God has dealt to each one a measure of faith."* (ROMANS 12:3)

If you put a car into a forward gear, it will go forward. If you put a car into reverse gear, it goes backwards. It all depends on how you use the gear lever. In the same way you can use your God-given ability positively and be in faith or negatively and be in fear; you cannot use it both ways at once. If you read through the Gospels, you will find that when people came to Jesus for help, He often told them that their faith had made them whole, or had saved them, or healed them. Faith will always find its way to Jesus. It attracts the goodness of God into your life. In the same way, fear attracts negative things into your life.

It is as true for us today as it was for Job, whose confession was that *"the thing I greatly feared has come upon me, and what I dreaded has happened to me".* (JOB 3:25)

What we fear can, and often will, happen to us. For example, if you fear cancer long enough, you may get it. I know people personally, who have had such a fear, and have been driven to their doctor so many times by it, only to be told after a thorough examination that they do not have cancer. However, with some, cancer has eventually been diagnosed. They finally got what they believed for! Of course the same truth applies to many other conditions besides cancer. Have you ever heard people say things like, "Oh, I always get a cold this time of the year" or "He was always weak as a child and he still is, poor thing"? You see, I believe that the power of our tongues can curse or bless us and those with whom we relate. So, we need to be very careful about what we say (Psalm 141:3), and make a real effort to be positive, unlike Job.

In other words just as faith attracts the good things of God into our life, fear attracts negative things. I trust that you understand and accept these spiritual principles. Until you are willing to face up to the whole area of positive and negative confession, the danger is that fear will control you.

Fear is negative and it attracts the negative. Faith is good and attracts the good. Your day to day experiences will depend on whether you are living in faith or fear. I counsel many people who are battling with depression and always find that they have areas of negative thinking. I was very impressed by a dictionary definition of depression that I read some years ago, which I think helps us to see the problem more clearly. The dictionary defined depression as a 'low spirit'. When a person is in low spirits they are afraid and worry anxiously about the things they do not want to happen to them. I once heard a psychiatrist describe fear as 'unintelligent thoughts whirling about in one's mind around a centre of fear.' He was right.

You see, we all get such attacks from time to time. I know that I do. I consider myself to be a positive person today but I have not always been that way. I used to be a chronic depressive on phenobarbitone tablets before I became a Christian, so I am speaking from personal experience. I still get attacked sometimes by 'unintelligent thoughts' that endeavour to influence my life. However, they can only stay if they can find a centre of fear to whirl around. As soon as I recognise them for what they are, I act by *"bringing every thought into captivity to the obedience of Christ"*. (2 CORINTHIANS 10:5)

Get to the point where you do the same. Remember, faith attracts the good things we want to happen to us, fear the bad. Whether you live with the good things or the bad things is your choice. Choose the Jesus way for the rest of your life and you will experience all the fullness and joy of the good things He has in store for you, His precious child.

Do Not Worry

"Therefore I say to you, do not worry about your life, what you will eat or what you will drink; nor about your body, what you will put on. Is not life more than food and the body more than clothing? Look at the birds of the air, for they neither sow nor reap nor gather into barns; yet your heavenly Father feeds them. Are you not of more value than they? Which of you by worrying can add one cubit to your stature? So why do you worry about clothing? Consider the lilies of the field, how they grow: they neither toil nor spin; and yet I say to you that even Solomon in all of his glory was not arrayed like one of these. Now if God so clothes the grass of the field, which today is, and tomorrow is thrown in the oven, will He not much more clothe you, O you of little faith? Therefore, do not worry, saying, "What shall we eat?" or "What shall we drink?" or "What shall we wear?" For after all these things the Gentiles seek. For your heavenly Father knows that you need all these things. But, seek first the kingdom of God and His righteousness, and all these things shall be added to you. Therefore, do not worry about tomorrow, for tomorrow will worry about its own things. Sufficient for the day is its own trouble." (MATTHEW 6:25-34)

So, God commands us not to worry and, therefore, to disobey is sin. So, if God gives a command, He does not tease us, He means it. If God says do something, it means that it is good for us to do it and also that you are capable of doing it, so be bold. I once heard an American preacher say, "If you worry you die, if you do not worry you die, so why worry?" We also read Paul telling us to, *"be anxious for nothing, but in everything by prayer and supplication, with thanksgiving, let your requests be made known to God."* (PHILIPPIANS 4:6)

So, do not be anxious. One of the recurring themes of the themes that I have tried to get across in the book is that there is no such thing as isolated depression, but that it always has a root cause somewhere, usually in something like fear or anxiety.

"Anxiety in the heart of man causes depression". (PROVERVBS 12:25)

So, instead of trying to treat the symptoms, we need to treat the root. Then the symptoms will take care of themselves and go. The Bible says 365 times 'be not afraid' or 'fear not' or something similar, so there is one for every day of the year. If it is a leap year, you can have a prophetic one of mine, 'do not worry'! Clearly the need is for you to exercise your will and decide, every day, not to worry. If you know you have not got the strength, do not be anxious but rather rejoice, because *'He (Jesus) said to me, "My grace is sufficient for you, for My strength is made perfect in weakness." Therefore, most gladly will I rather boast in my infirmities, that the power of Christ may rest upon me. Therefore, I take pleasure in infirmities, in reproaches, in needs, in persecutions, in distresses, for Christ's sake. For when I am weak, then I am strong.'* (2 CORINTHIANS 12:9-10)

I can tell you I have been attacked by fear many more times than I care to remember. Sometimes I can almost feel it making progress and getting control over me if I allow it to persist. But, when I realise what is happening and stand up against it and begin to attack it with the word of God and confess 'it's the truth that sets me free', the fear soon begins to withdraw and before long, it's gone.

A friend of mine made this statement, "worry is unholy meditation". Another friend once said, "fear is the darkroom in which your negatives are developed". Even more to the point, I heard somebody else say that "anxiety is a vote of no-confidence in the reign of the Lord Jesus Christ".

Let these quotations motivate you to say no to fear, worry and anxiety and yes to Jesus and His promises of good things for those who love Him.

Into the Deep End

I want to say that in writing about anxiety, I am basing a lot of what I am saying not simply upon the word of God and what has happened to those I have ministered to over the years, but upon my own personal experience. Some folks may say, 'It is all right for you, you're a strong man of God, but what do you know about the way I have suffered all these years?' So, let me give you a little testimony of how I was freed from the realm of anxiety and fear when I came to Christ.

Until fairly recently I had a dreadful fear of water, and I am now in my sixties. I was prayed for by many people, and over the years by many people with well-known deliverance 'ministries', but nothing ever changed. I have been a Christian for 40 years, and for 32 years of my walk I had lived with this debilitating fear of water. It was so bad that I experienced severe stress every time I had my hair washed, because the worst part of it was that I could not bear water to get around my face. In fact, all those years I usually had to get somebody to wash my hair for me, while I covered my face tightly with a towel.

Then, one day a colleague of mine had a word of knowledge from God while he was praying for me. So, he immediately phoned me up and said, "God has shown me how this fear of water got into you." So I said, "You'd better get around here quickly and pray for me". He came straight round and prayed for me and the fear instantly left me, praise the Lord!

Also, just to prove that Satan no longer had a hold on me, and that I had been totally delivered by the blood of Jesus, I went down a 70-foot water shoot into the deep end at a leisure pool, and I cannot even swim, but I had no fear! My daughter was there with a video camera to record it. *"I sought the Lord and He heard me and delivered me from all my fears".* (PSALM 34:4)

It may be that I have not touched on your particular fear in this chapter, or even the root of your fear. I believe, though, that the Lord knows exactly what your needs are right at this moment. Please pray that He will show you exactly what can be done to set you free in the areas that He has highlighted, or you have become aware of as you read this book. If you have someone to whom you can turn to be alongside you at this time, then please ask them to come and pray with you. Let me leave this chapter with the thought that where Jesus is fear cannot be, because *"there is no fear in love; but perfect love casts out fear"*. (1 JOHN 4:18)

So, remain in Him always by soaking yourself in the Bible and by praying, and each and every fear will be forced out and will have to stay out.

❈ ❈ ❈

CHAPTER 6

FACING FAILURE

The account of Jesus and Peter walking on the water is one of my favourites, because it contains so much truth and so many good examples for us of the nature of Jesus. I want to use it now to point out to you some things that will equip you to have the victory over anxiety, fear, worry and failure.

"*Immediately Jesus made His disciples get into the boat and go before Him to the other side, while He sent the multitudes away. And when He had sent the multitudes away, He went up on the mountain by Himself to pray. Now when evening came, He was alone there. But, the boat was now in the middle of the sea, tossed by the waves, for the wind was contrary. Now in the fourth watch of the night Jesus went to them, walking on the sea. And when the disciples saw Him walking on the sea, they were troubled, saying, 'It is a ghost!' and they cried out for fear. But, immediately Jesus spoke to them, saying, 'Be of good cheer! It is I; do not be afraid.' and Peter answered Him and said, 'Lord, if it is You, command me to come to You on the water.' So, He said, 'Come,' and when Peter had come down out of the boat, he walked on the water to go to Jesus. But, when he saw that the wind was boisterous, he was afraid; and beginning to sink he cried out, saying, 'Lord, save me!' and immediately Jesus stretched out His hand and caught him, and said to him, 'O you of little faith, why did you doubt?' and when they got into the boat, the wind ceased. Then those who were in the boat came and worshipped Him, saying, 'truly You are the Son of God'*". (MATTHEW 14:22-33)

Jesus had told the disciples to get into a boat and put to sea. At first they made good progress but soon a storm blew up and the weather deteriorated until they could see nothing ahead of them but a watery grave. Later, in the fourth watch of the night, something happened. That time between 2am and 4am is the darkest and most fearful time of the night. If, like me, you have been through times of depression, you will know it well. It was during this time that Jesus appeared. Did you know that you can meet Him at your darkest hour? He is always there and in fact it is His speciality. I often say that Jesus' address is No1, Wit's End Corner.

Fear sees Ghosts, Faith sees Jesus
Jesus came to his disciples while they were still in the middle of the lake, and their reaction was to cry out in fear, thinking He was a ghost. Both Matthew and Mark agree in their accounts of this event that the disciples had already forgotten the feeding of over five thousand people with a little boy's lunch. One of the greatest miracles, especially for the disciples who had been so closely involved in the feeding of the crowd, had happened less than twelve hours before and now they did not even recognise Jesus! Fear never recognises truth; it only sees ghosts.

Having got over the initial panic, Peter, the impetuous one, said, "Lord, if it is you, command me to come to you on the water". Jesus simply replied, "Come". That one word was enough for Peter, so he got out of the boat and began to walk across the water to Jesus. It is interesting that he asked Jesus to command him rather than ask him; perhaps he remembered the effect of Jesus' commands on previous occasions.

Peter was a human being just like you and me, he had his own fears (see Matthew 26:74), and was also confused (see Mark 9:6). But he was still willing to get out of the boat and walk on the water. Note that the storm did not die away as Peter stepped out of the boat. He had to step into the storm and walk over an angry sea. Many depressed people would like God to take the storms out of their lives and make the sea as calm as a millpond for them; but that is rarely the way God works. Often, He will not take our problems away from us but will always enable us to triumph over them by faith. The Christian life does not guarantee us perpetual calm weather but it does provide victory in time of rough weather.

When Peter stepped out of the boat he made good progress while he kept his eyes and his faith fixed on Jesus. When he looked away and became aware of his circumstances, though, he began to sink. Peter started to look at the waves, listen to the wind, feel the spray on his body and smell the water; in other words he began to move from 'faith knowledge' to 'sense knowledge'. Some people say we should use our common sense because God gave it to us, and so He did, but He does not ask us to live by it! The Bible says on four separate occasions, *"the just shall live by faith"*, which cannot mean by common sense. Common sense would never get out of a boat and try to walk on the water!

Peter went back to his sense knowledge, his feelings and his emotions, and he began to relate to his environment more than to his teacher. When he did that, he began to sink. Many people go into a swift emotional spiral towards depression by the same route. They turn away from Jesus, His word and His promises and begin to relate to what is going on around them.

That Sinking Feeling

Peter, however, gives us a tremendous example of how to react, which is why I love this passage so much. You see, when he began to sink, he did not wait until he was going down for the third time and then panic, but he **immediately** cried out to the Lord for help. Follow Peter's example! Giving in to that sinking feeling is an indication that we are beginning to allow our circumstances to preach to us instead of listening to the word of God. At that moment, you are in great danger of falling into the sin of trusting your own strength, which will always fail you.

Another danger signal is when you begin to attend a self-worship service rather than a God centered worship service. This will often reveal itself as an attack of the POM's (Poor Old Me's), a sure sign you have forgotten the promises of God and the fact that you are one of His favourite children. Are you really aware of this truth? I have five children. Do you know which is the favourite? All five! To me they are the finest children in the world and I am proud of them all. God has a big family of favourite children and you and I are in it. If you remember that and believe it, you will never have an excuse for an attack of the P.O.M.'s again.

A further signal of distress is the emergence of a 'chip' on one's shoulder. I find it is often expressed in the question, "Why does it always happen to me?" When someone asks me that question, I usually reply with the verse, *"Trust in the Lord with all your heart, and lean not on your own understanding"* (PROVERBS 3:5), and remind them *"that all things work together for good to those who love God, to those who are the called according to His purpose".* (ROMANS 8:28)

Peter's reaction when he began to sink illustrates another tremendous lesson for us. Many people, when they begin to feel that they are a failure, also begin to feel condemned. They then try to fight off the depression and work their way out of it in their own strength. They grit their teeth and do their best, but it is never good enough, because you cannot 'work' your way out of depression or failure. Peter did not fall into that trap. He was an experienced fisherman and knew all about the 'normal' properties of water; he was very well aware that you should not be able to walk on it. He was also aware that even though you can swim in it, it was stormy. He did not even try. That would have been self-effort. He just called out to Jesus for help.

Wise Words
The Lord's reaction to Peter sinking encourages me too. I am glad He did not rebuke or accuse him, or send him home to live miserably for a week or two before he was forgiven. Neither did He pick Peter up and carry him back to the boat. That is what a lot of people would like to happen when they go into depression, but Jesus will not do it. He took Peter by the hand, and it was as though he was saying, 'come on Peter, stand up on the water. We are going to walk back to the boat together'. That is how to live in victory over failure: let Jesus take you by the hand and walk with you on top of your circumstances and problems.

When Peter got back into the boat he was wet, tired and probably feeling a failure, but Jesus did not tell him off for sinking. I'm thrilled about that, because it shows so clearly God's character. A man might say to me, "It serves you right", but I do not live by what I deserve. I live by grace, which is 'something for nothing for those who do not deserve anything'. I know my Father and I know He loves me. He never gives me what I am due, because I know that I only deserve punishment. I live in His grace and so can enjoy all the things I do not deserve.

You Have Enough Faith!
When they did eventually get back to the boat, Jesus simply said, "O you of little faith". You might think that was a discouraging remark, but I find there is something encouraging about it too. You see, it tells me that you

can walk on water with only a little faith. I am sure that some of you, as you have been reading this, have been saying to yourselves, "I do not have enough faith to lead that kind of life, which is why I become afraid and feel such a failure. I will never have enough faith". Well, if you have only a very little faith, it is enough to enable you to walk on the water, and I do not think God has asked you to do anything as hard as that! You certainly have enough faith to live above fear, worry, failure and depression—so you can live above your circumstances. *"As God has dealt to each one a measure of faith".* (ROMANS 12:3)

The day I first believed that it is possible to walk on water with only a little faith was, I think, one of the greatest revelations I have ever received from God. The problem for many of us is that we do not use the faith we do have. When we begin to do so, we can live by it and know complete victory over our circumstances. Jesus said, that *"if you have faith as a mustard seed, you will say to this mountain, 'move from here to there', and it will move".* (MATTHEW 17:20)

But, many Christians think that it is only when they have faith like a mountain that they might just about be able to move a mustard seed! Notice that after Peter had begun to fail and had called out to Jesus for help, he walked on the water again! His last memory of the episode was one of victoriously walking back to the boat with Jesus. No Christian needs to be a permanent failure, because our Saviour takes our failures and turns them into stepping stones to success!

An African Tale

I have shown that fear plays a major part in the lives of many people today but we have seen that the fear does not come from God. The Bible tells us that, *"God has not given us a spirit of fear, but of power and of love and of a sound mind."* (2 TIMOTHY 1:7)

Instead of dwelling on our fears, which do not come from God, we should dwell on what He has given us: love, power and a sound mind. Spend some time meditating on these three promises and see the Lord change the way you think about yourself.

Finally, let me encourage you with a story from Africa one of my team heard recently. A group of men walked a long way from their tribal village to hear the Gospel preached for the first time. They set off back to their homes saved and excited with God's touch on their lives. When they were almost back, they found that it had rained and a dry watercourse had become a swiftly moving river, at least ¼ mile wide, blocking their way. With no materials to construct a raft, the men were seriously concerned about how they could reach their village.

Suddenly, one of the men recalled the passage that the speaker at the crusade had preached on—it was the account of Jesus and Peter walking on the water. They felt they should do the same, so they stepped out onto the waters in faith. Within a few minutes they had crossed the river! Unbeknown to them, some of their neighbours had watched, amazed, as the men crossed over. They ran back to tell the village, and the men were able to testify about Jesus immediately they entered the village. As a result, everyone in the village gave their lives to the Lord. Praise God.

What a faith building story! I know that we may never have to find the faith to do something so wonderful, but we still need the faith we have been given to live victoriously day by day. If you only remember one thing from this chapter, let it be that Peter called out immediately he started to sink and that Jesus responded to that cry immediately and with real compassion. His desire is to meet you at your point of need, so do not let feelings of failure escalate and become depression by waiting before you call out to Him. Do it straight away so you can get back into all the fullness He wants you to enjoy.

❈ ❈ ❈

CHAPTER 7

BREAK FREE FROM STRESS

"Oh, I'm under so much stress at the moment!" This is a common excuse people use to explain why they are not coping with life. Providing stress management courses is big business today. In America, for example, one popular image is of a nation of people dependant upon their therapists. Many men no longer feel secure in their jobs. They may fear someone being brought in to replace them, the threat of redundancy or years of unemployment stretching ahead of them. Many people live under this sort of cloud every day. Some employers are able to get their employees to work longer hours with no overtime pay, simply by the unspoken threat of competition for their post. If this is you, or you feel under the bondage of stress in your life for any other reason, the good news is you do not have to stay there. Jesus is the answer to your situation and is calling out to you to let Him change your circumstances around to a life of victory. He came *"to set at liberty those who are oppressed"*. (LUKE 4:18)

A Merry Heart

"A merry heart does good like medicine, but a broken spirit dries the bones". (PROVERBS 17:22)

Did you know that medical science in this century has proved this verse to be true? They have discovered that major causes of arthritis are bitterness, resentment, unforgiveness and holding grudges, because they dry up the fluid that lubricates the joints. These are not the only causes of arthritis though, so do not start thinking that this is the complete answer. However, it could be, and so may need your prayerful consideration. Isn't it amazing, "a broken spirit dries up the bones"?

But, praise the Lord that it is a scriptural fact that "a merry heart does good like medicine". In other words, healing can, and will, come through joy.

I will never forget the Christmas when I heard somebody say, "I really believe that all Christians should be wishing each other a MERRY Christmas", because up to that point I thought we should not do that. Since becoming a Christian myself, I considered merriment to be linked with the worldly concept of having drinks, getting drunk and being out of control. I believe now, though, that you can go and get a drink at the 'New Jerusalem Public House', and have a good dram of the Spirit of God. In fact, until you have been drunk in the Spirit, you have not enjoyed the fullness of scripture! When the 120 walked out from the upper room at Pentecost, those on the streets said "they are full of new wine". It looked like they were drunk, and in fact they were, but it was with the new wine of the Holy Spirit! (ACTS 2:13)

The truth is that Jesus has got great things planned for us (John 10:10). Attitudes that make us sombre and serious can bring ill-health to us. Being gloomy, downcast or plain miserable, is not how we should behave, especially when we are meant to be in love with the Lord Jesus Christ. I often say, "you show me a Christian without joy, and I will show you a weak one, but you show me a Christian who is bubbling with joy and I will show you a strong one". You see, a Christian without joy is like Samson with a haircut! *"For the joy of the Lord is our strength"*. (NEHEMIAH 8:10)

Be Enthusiastic

Do you know what the word 'enthusiastic' means? It comes from a Greek word that has been transplanted into English. I have discovered that the Greeks had no word for excitement about God, so they had to invent a new word. What they came up with was 'en-theos', or enthuse. A more literal translation from the Greek is, 'to be violently alive in God'. I think that some of us would do well to get some of this type of godly joy and become violently alive in God. We British can be too formal, too religious and too bound up. We need to be set free and let the joy of God flow, like a river. Then we can experience the strength and the healing that the Word says will follow.

I really do believe that we need real physical joy to be released in us because in it there is healing. Let me say that again so there is no confusion, THERE IS HEALTH IN JOY AND IN GIVING PRAISE TO OUR FATHER IN HEAVEN. The more joy we have, the more health we will have. *"A merry heart does good like medicine".* (PROVERBS 17:22)

If you are saying to yourself that you cannot be joyful because of the stressful situation you're in, read on. If you really love the Lord and you want to become free, He will equip you to reach the point of freedom you desire. Remember, He wants you to be free too.

Facts not Feelings
I know of a woman, an American, who was remarkably changed by just such a regular confession. She was challenged when she confessed to her Pastor that she did not feel loved by God or anyone else, and he replied "Do not listen to your feelings, but believe the facts about how God thinks about you". Her response was to set herself the task of speaking out loud, "Jesus lives in me", 200 times every day. Even when she may have forgotten to do it for a few days, she refused to give up.

Guess what happened after six months? Right! She knew with absolute conviction, in a way that no person could shake her from, that Jesus did indeed live in her. It totally transformed her life. Today she lives in the freedom that comes from knowing Jesus intimately in her life every minute, because of the disciplined routine she set herself. Why not do the same? Ask the Lord to give you a scripture to confess and see the difference in the coming weeks and months. Believe, and you will see your life change, literally before your eyes.

The important thing to remember though is that the Lord will act in His time schedule. When there appears to be little or no change and you feel like giving up, get back to the Bible, stand on the promises, and then stand on them some more. Your faith for a complete change in your circumstances will be built up as you continually confess the Truth, for *"faith comes by hearing, and hearing by the word of God".* (ROMANS 10:17)

Experience CANNOT Nullify the Word
Let me give you an example from my own recent experience to show the necessity of standing firmly on the word whatever the circumstances. I had to preach at the funeral of a member of my team; his name was Ron Guy.

A cancerous tumour developed in his brain, and in a very short time it killed him. Now, I know that Ron had prayed for the sick on many occasions, I was often with him when he did so, and had seen God do many amazing things, he even saw a dead person raised back to life. But, although many people prayed for him when he was ill, he still died.

I emphasised one thing at his funeral—that Ron would be furious with anybody who said that they could not be healed by God, by comparing their situation with his. He would have been very angry if anyone had said, "Look, Ron did not get healed, so I cannot get healed!". Ron was a man of the word, "which is forever settled in Heaven", and he would always say that God's word is totally sufficient for every situation. ANOTHER PERSON'S EXPERIENCE CANNOT NULLIFY THE WORD OF GOD.

Everything the Bible says is the truth, Hallelujah! I am going to preach that truth uncompromisingly. If everybody I pray for dies, I am still going to believe the Word, because my Bible says that God heals the sick. *"My son give attention to my words, incline your ear to sayings, do not let them depart from your eyes, keep them in the midst of your heart, for they are life to those who find them, and health to all their flesh."* (PROVERBS 4:20-22)

A Positive Confession

Another problem area can arise when we are hard and critical of ourselves. Negative attitudes will produce an environment that will breed depression and stress in you and others. A positive confession, though, will gradually promote an environment conducive to health and freedom from anything that is gripping your life. A Christian should become disciplined enough to make a regular, positive confession about their physical or spiritual condition, firmly grounded in the word of God. When they begin to speak the truth about themselves based upon the way God thinks and feels about them, their whole situation will begin to change. *"Pleasant words are like a honeycomb, sweetness to the soul and health to the bones".* (PROVERBS 16:29)

So, pleasant words give health to other people's bones as well as our own. Knowing this to be true, do you really want to curse another person's bones and bring darkness to their soul by being negative about them or saying negative things to them? The answer surely is no you do not, and that if you have not got anything pleasant to say, do not say anything at all! On the other hand, isn't it good just to encourage one another with pleasant words, especially as you now know that when you are doing it, you are giving health to that mind and body?

You see, we sometimes miss these less well known verses about healing, and only remember ones like, *"they shall lay hands on the sick, and they shall recover"*. (MARK 16:18)

That is the favourite one, isn't it? But, verses like Proverbs 16:17 show that there are other issues that throw light on the reasons why some people do not get healed. There are some people who, every time you see them, moan and groan and complain and are full of misery; nothing is ever right, everything is always wrong, and other people are always to blame for their misfortunes. Is it any wonder they are sick?

We so easily let our circumstances change our confession. We need to live with pleasant words in our mouths all the time, and the time to start speaking these pleasant words is, I believe, when you first open your mouth in the morning. Those who know me know that the first person I meet in a new day is greeted with, "It's the greatest day you ever lived!" because I really mean it. Yesterday is gone, tomorrow is not here yet, we've only got today, so we might as well praise the Lord in it. This is the day that the Lord has made for me to rejoice and be glad in, and I refuse to insult Him by using the day that He made for moaning and groaning and complaining and getting negative. Remember, the moment you begin praising God, as well as encouraging others by your enthusiasm, you have got some healing in your bones.

Promote Health

"Death and life are in the power of the tongue and those who love it will eat its fruit". (PROVERBS 18:21)

"There is one who speaks like the piercing of a sword, but the tongue of the wise promotes health". (PROVERBS 12:18)

You can promote health. You can promote death. So, when you meet somebody, think about the effect your meeting will have on them. If you say something to them that is wise, you're promoting health in them. You see, you do not have to have what many call a 'healing ministry' to bring healing to people. What you can do is to go around promoting health in people by saying wise and encouraging things to them. Lift them up with wisdom.

The world is in an awful state around us, and there are not many people saying wise things. In fact, I believe we need to be vigilant to guard ourselves so that things that are contrary to scripture do not take root in our minds. For example, I heard someone on the television recently saying sin does not offend God. He was relating it specifically to Prince Charles' adultery. I shouted out straight away, "It DOES offend God!" You see, I was refusing to let that seed of untruth come into my mind. Denying God's word in that way is exactly the sort of thing that can eventually allow sin, deception, sickness and depression to come into people's lives.

You may think that this is going over the top, but I disagree. Joshua 1:8 speaks about meditating on the Word of God 'day and night'. It is in the Bible, so it must be possible to attain this level of holiness. God's desire is for the word to dwell in us all the time, and for 'good' reason. The good reason is, to keep the 'world' out, and especially to keep us from being yoked to it. We have to live in the world, but Peter says we are aliens (1 Peter 2:11), so let's act like we are.

You may feel a little daunted by the prospect of changing so many behaviour patterns in order to put my suggestions from the Bible into practice. Let me encourage you to persevere. It will take a lifetime to put on the list in Galations 5:22-23, but God calls us to do just that, 'put them on'. As I understand it, that means it is possible! Be merry and speak positively. If you manage to put both into operation as part of your daily discipline, then no stress-related illness will ever be able to come and take root in you again

CHAPTER 8

FEELING SECURE

"He gives them security, and they rely on it; yet His eyes are on their ways". (JOB 24:23)

The roots of all the areas I am tackling in this book are to be found in the day to day experiences of peoples' lives. Hurts are caused both deliberately and accidentally, wounds are received knowingly and unexpectedly. But the common factor is that our minds tend to cope by locking these hurts away. Our characters can then become altered as we teach ourselves to steer clear of situations where we may be hurt in the same way again. The good news is that Jesus took all of our hurts to the cross, and that in His resurrection He made it possible for us to experience complete freedom in Him in our daily walk.

A Personal Testimony

I was a father with five children before I become aware of the consequences of a temporary break in my own family relationships that occurred when I was a lad. My elder sister had died when she was two weeks old, and as I was the only other child in the family, it is not surprising that my parents were very protective and concerned for my welfare. When they discovered that I had tubercular glands (which at that time was a very serious condition) they were devastated.

My parents took me to hospital where I was to undergo surgery and handed me over to a nurse who, quite abruptly, took me away from them. As she did so I felt a sudden insecurity, and began to scream at the top of my voice. My mother told me, many years later, that as they left the building they could still hear me. Children were not allowed visitors at that time, so it was a month before I saw either of my parents again. It was

51

only as an adult that I found out that that incident had been tucked away at the back of my memory, and I did not realise how much it had affected my life.

What made me aware of what had happened was hearing a man, whose ministry I greatly respect, speaking on Isaiah Chapter 53. He read, *"He is despised and rejected by men, a man of sorrows and acquainted with grief. And we hid, as it were, our faces from Him; He was despised, and we did not esteem Him. Surely He has borne our griefs and carried our sorrows; yet we esteemed Him stricken, smitten by God, and afflicted. But He was wounded for our transgressions, He was bruised for our iniquities; the chastisement for our peace was upon Him, and by His stripes we are healed."* (Isaiah 53:3-5)

Like myself, that man believed that these verses could be applied to physical healing. However, on this occasion he stressed their relevance to the damaging effects of past emotional wounds, from which we need to be set free. We might not realise it but these wounds are often the root causes of why we react badly in certain circumstances. Too often we excuse a bad attitude or behaviour by saying, 'That is just the way I am'. The preacher suggested that some of his listeners might have put up with such conditions in ignorance for many years, in which case it was time to see that Jesus had indeed provided healing for us through His wounds on the cross. Then, through repentance, we could receive our healing by faith.

This really hit home for me, because although I am normally a secure person, there were times when I would be overwhelmed by sudden feelings of insecurity that I did not understand, and which caused me to react badly. That night, after the meeting, I discussed the problem with my wife, Heather, who agreed that I did have these feelings of insecurity. She also declared that God did not want me to continue that way.

As we waited upon the Lord, He reminded me of the time when I had suddenly been 'abandoned' and showed me that this was the root of my insecurity. As I looked to the cross and saw Jesus being wounded there for me, I repented of carrying the hurt for so long. Heather prayed with me, asking the Lord to release and heal me. I was wonderfully changed. I felt like a completely new man and can best describe the experience as similar to being saved all over again. There has been a permanent and radical change in my life for which I only give glory to God. Jesus knows it is only the anointing of God that can set us completely free from these things. He said, *"The Spirit of the LORD is upon Me, because He has anointed Me to preach the gospel to the poor; He has sent Me to heal the brokenhearted, to proclaim liberty to the captives and recovery of sight to the blind, to set at liberty those who are oppressed".* (LUKE 4:18)

Jesus heals people with broken hearts and sets them free. He releases those who are bound by insecurity and sets them free. He removes the effects of emotional wounds from the past and sets the victims free. The Apostle Peter exhorts us to *"throw the whole weight of your anxieties upon Him, for you are His personal concern".* (1 PETER 5:7 JB PHILLIPS)

God loves you, He is personally concerned about you and wants you to be completely free from every insecurity in your life.

God has Faith in You!

I was ministering in America a few years ago in a big church with hundreds of members, which regularly had visiting preachers. I was preaching at one of the morning services where you only get a small crowd but, none the less, many folks came forward for prayer. As I was praying for them, I came to this lady who was a chronic depressant. As I prayed for her, I suddenly realised I was about to become another in a long list of itinerants who had prayed for her to no effect. So I lifted my heart to the Lord and asked for a word for that lady. Straight away the Lord told me to tell her, "I have got faith in you". That was suddenly a problem for me, because throughout my ministry I had been telling people that they needed to have faith in God, and now God was asking me to tell this woman that He had faith in her!

Anyway, I did as I was told. The moment I spoke the words, her eyes began to sparkle, her face lit up and she began to smile for apparently the first time in ages. I prayed for her, and before sending her home, asked the Lord for a verse to back up the word that He had given me. He reminded me of this passage, *"You did not choose me, but I chose you and appointed you that you shall go and bear fruit, and that your fruit shall remain, that whatever you ask the Father in my name He may give you."* (JOHN 15:16)

That morning, God showed me that the people who come into His Kingdom, do not come because they choose to enter, but because He

53

chooses them. He chose each one of us because He has got faith in us! Someone once shared a paraphrase with me that I really like, "God has handpicked you".

I was told after the meeting that the lady used to lie in bed all day, too depressed to do anything. Her husband had to come home and clean the house, cook the food, look after the children and do virtually everything. But things quickly changed. On the day of her healing, when her husband came home from work, the house was clean, there was a hot meal cooked, and ready to go on the plate for him. Her husband was a non-Christian and was really impressed with the changes in her. It was not long before he began to attend Church. Isn't it amazing that the lady was wonderfully set free by that simple word.

I want you to know that God has got faith in you too, so there's no need for you to worry about anything. He cares about you and you are His personal concern. *"Be anxious for nothing, but in everything by prayer and supplication, with thanksgiving, let your requests be made known to God."* (PHILIPPIANS 4:6)

My friend Mike Darwood puts it like this: if he asks someone, "How are you?" and the reply is, "Oh, I'm fine, under the circumstances", (quite a common phrase that you possibly have spoken many times), Mike will then say to them, "What are you doing under your circumstances when, in Christ, you should be living over your circumstances?" So, are you living under or over your circumstances? Let me assure you, it is possible to live on top of them. I live over them, and I know many others who do too. Simply let God reign in every area of your life and you too will experience living 'on top of the world'.

Practically, in terms of regular Christian discipline, God's plan is for you to bring your whole life into relationship with Him, through prayer, meditation and worship. But, in every prayer-time, for example, it is far more important for you to hear what God is saying to you, than to bring Him a 'shopping list' of needs and wants. When you bring your requests to God in the light of your relationship with Him, He will speak to you through this relationship, and you will walk in freedom with the Lord. Crucially, this will develop your relationship with Him to the point where you really do not have to be anxious ever again.

God's Feelings for You
If you know beyond any shadow of a doubt that God loves you, I do not believe you will ever get depressed. Sadly many people have no such assurance. They are not convinced that God loves them, and because of that they have no assurance that He has accepted them. The Bible says, *"We love Him because He first loved us"*. (1 JOHN 4:19)

But it is not sufficient for me to tell you that God loves you. It might persuade you intellectually but that is not enough. I thank God, though, that I have something more than an intellectual persuasion that God loves me. I no longer have to go to the Bible to prove it, I know He does. You see, I *"know the love of Christ which passes knowledge"* (EPHESIANS 3:19); even though it is a contradiction to the natural mind. How can we know the love of God which, according to the verse I have just quoted, cannot be known? The glorious truth is that we can know this love as a reality in our lives through an intimate relationship with the person who is the fullest expression of that love to the world, Jesus Christ. Although we can never grasp it intellectually, God loves us beyond words and we can experience it through His Son. The God who made this universe actually takes up residence in our lives, by the Holy Spirit, and makes us aware of His presence and His love. When John Wesley said 'my heart was strangely warmed', I am sure he was saying that he felt and knew the love of God inside him.

I have no time for the brand of Christianity that I call 'believerism', which is really only the power of 'mind over matter'. It tries to persuade people to believe in God because the Bible says so, while totally ignoring their feelings. I believe that feelings are important, and that it is impossible to have Jesus Christ in your life and not feel He is there. The Bible does not present a 'no feelings' brand of Christianity. I am convinced that God wants us to really know that He loves us. He wants us to fully experience His love, for only then can we totally respond to Him. People who have never experienced God's love in this way can only offer Him an intellectual love in return.

I believe strongly that it is the lack of a deep and total love relationship with God which leaves people wide open to insecurity, fear and anxiety. I do not get upset when people I am counselling become emotional and the tears begin to flow, in fact I like to see it happen. It was not Satan who made our emotions but God, and love is an emotion and He is love. I have no time for emotionalism, but emotions are good. Real security only comes from that relationship with God in which we know that He loves us. Let me encourage you to read 1 John every day for the next week or two and let the fullest expression of God's love in the Bible become more and more real in your life.

Express It
God does not want us to just tell people that He loves them. He wants us to be His love to them. There is tremendous security in God's family, the Body of Christ, as we experience God's love flowing from one to another, and learn to trust each other. I have no problem in relating to a brother or sister if I know that they love me and they know that I love them. On that basis, nothing that either of us may do will destroy our relationship. Our love does not depend on doing everything right; it is, in fact, when we make mistakes that the love of others is most needed, and, I've found in my personal experience, most expressed. I find such security in the knowledge that if I make a mistake I will not be rejected by family, team or friends, but will receive the correction I need at that moment out of the love we have for each other. We read that, *"if a brother or sister is naked, and destitute of daily food, and one of you says to them, 'depart in peace, be warmed and filled,' but you do not give them the things that are needed for the body, what does it profit?"* (JAMES 2:15-16).

In other words, James is saying it is not simply enough to tell a person that you love them, you have to demonstrate to him that you do. A lack of love can lead to loneliness, rejection, insecurity, fear, resentfulness and eventually depression. Fullness of God's love brings security, peace, joy and bright hope for the future in Him.

I hope that I have managed to convey the centrality of your love relationship with Jesus to God's plan for releasing you from your insecurities. I have shown through my testimony how a person can be unknowingly affected by things from their past. Your mind may throw some memories out, but it can bury others deeply which will remain to influence you. Jesus, though, is both able and willing to amputate and throw away every fear, worry and insecurity you may be burdened with. Remember, His will is that you should live in freedom and He can bring you into that freedom if you ask Him. Your job is to accept and receive His love and make every effort, through prayer and reading the word, to build up your love for Him more and more.

❈ ❈ ❈

CHAPTER 9

YOU CAN DO IT!

Having finished the book, I pray that you have already begun to find peace and freedom through the truth of God's word. Let me encourage you, as you begin your 'new' life, to make every effort to remain equipped to walk in victory. So, having cleared out a lot of rubbish, it is important to fill yourself with as much of God as you can. Ask Him to fill you completely full of the Holy Spirit right now and do the same every morning for the rest of your life. Ask Him to reveal how pleased He is that you have got rid of that which hindered, to enable you to love and serve Him better from this day onward. Ask Him to show you the way He desires you to go in your new life with Him. Some of you may know such a release, for example, that you will be able to take up the call to full-time ministry, or make yourself available to your Church for a task that needs your help.

The enormous relief you can experience through knowing complete freedom in the areas I have covered may last a week or a year or a lifetime. The length of time you remain in the blessing, though, depends upon the priority you give God in your life from now on. If you choose to, you can remain in His blessing for ever, or only 10 minutes, it's up to you. You may have heard some people say, "I put God first, my wife second, the children third, church fourth, work fifth and self last". I used to say the same until the Lord revealed the truth that the Bible reveals on this matter. You see, one of the names for God that we find in the book of Revelation is "the Alpha and the Omega, the First and the Last". God showed me that we must put Him first and second and third and last. When we manage to do this, all the other concerns of our lives; like family, church and work will be completely taken care of. In relation to the things we have been looking at in this book, think about the impact of putting God first in everything you are and everything you do. There will be no time to be worried about failing, to be anxious, to become stressed or insecure, to be fearful or depressed or suffer from any other related issue. You see, He will cover and protect you 24 hours a day through the power of His love, and you, as you become more and more like Jesus through the development of this daily relationship, will become stronger and stronger in your faith, until you will eventually be able to help others who are where you used to be.

However, I must tell you that you will be tempted to believe that you are not actually free at all, or that when the good feelings wear off that is the end of your healing. So, just remember that when God sets us free, we are free indeed! But, temptation is coming, so arm yourself (Ephesians 6:13-17). Deal with Satan when he whispers in your ear, in the way it hurts him most by using the name of Jesus. The Holy Spirit will also equip and empower you to deal with the enemy too, so practice listening to Jesus' voice in your prayer times now, so that you will be able to recognise it when you need to in the future.

Finally, practice the good patterns I have highlighted throughout the book. Speak wisdom to your friends as well as to your non-Christian colleagues. Get into positive confession about every circumstance in your life: job, husband, wife, children, Church, homegroup, health, prayer, finances, Bible-study and so on. Notice that both these disciplines are about SPEAKING OUT LOUD. I have referred several times in the book to the power and authority of the tongue. Words are important: God SPOKE creation into being and SPOKE through the Prophets, Jesus SPOKE healing and life to dead bodies, and QUOTED the Old Testament to Satan to counter temptation. Our words also 'have the power of life or death', so, get into the habit of speaking the promises of God out loud every day. Then you will begin to believe that they are the truth for your situation.

Study and meditate on the Word 'day and night' and search the Bible when you need to find out God's opinion on something. Ask a Christian friend by all means, but get into the habit of doing it yourself too. Be merry at all times, not just at Christmas and birthdays, and ask to be filled with the Holy Spirit at the start of every day. Believe that each new day will bring good things and a fresh revelation of the Lord.

It will take real discipline to establish patterns like these, but I can tell you they will soon become second nature to you as you begin to reap the good from what you are sowing in your life. Finally, here is a promise for you to hold onto, the truth to set, and keep, you free. *"If God is for us, who can be against us?".* (Romans 8:31)